21st Century
Basic Skills
Library

I KNOW SOCCER

by Joanne Mattern

Cherry Lake Publishing • Ann Arbor, Michigan

3

Published in the United States of America
by Cherry Lake Publishing
Ann Arbor, Michigan
www.cherrylakepublishing.com

Consultant: Marla Conn, Read-Ability

Photo Credits: iStockphoto/Thinkstock, cover, 1; Maxisport/Shutterstock
Images, 4, 20; Andreas Gradin/Shutterstock Images, 6; AP Images, 8;
Rafael Ramirez Lee/Shutterstock Images, 10; Alex Menendez/AP Images,
12; Brocreative/Shutterstock Images, 14; Amy Myers/Shutterstock Images,
16; Robert J. Beyers II/Shutterstock Images, 18

Copyright ©2014 by Cherry Lake Publishing
All rights reserved. No part of this book may be reproduced or utilized in
any form or by any means without written permission from the publisher.

Library of Congress Cataloging-in-Publication Data
Mattern, Joanne, 1963-
  I know soccer / Joanne Mattern.
     pages cm. -- (I know sports)
  ISBN 978-1-62431-402-5 (hardcover) -- ISBN 978-1-62431-478-0 (pbk.) --
ISBN 978-1-62431-440-7 (pdf) -- ISBN 978-1-62431-516-9 (ebook)
1. Soccer--Juvenile literature. I. Title.
  GV943.25.M296 2013
  796.334--dc23
                                              2013008485

Cherry Lake Publishing would like to acknowledge
the work of The Partnership for 21st Century Skills.
Please visit www.p21.org for more information.

Printed in the United States of America
Corporate Graphics Inc.
July 2013
CLFA11

TABLE OF CONTENTS

History

Soccer has two names. It is called football in most countries. It is called soccer in the United States.

People have played soccer for almost 200 years. It is the most **popular** sport in the world.

Soccer teams from around the world play in the World Cup. It is a **tournament** played every four years. The first World Cup was in 1930.

Playing the Game

Soccer is played on a big field. There are two teams. Each team has a goal at one end of the field.

Players pass the ball to each other. They try to score in the other team's goal. A **goalie** tries to block the ball.

Soccer players do not need much **equipment**. Cleats and shin guards are all they need.

Rules

Players pass the ball mostly with their feet. They may not use their hands or arms.

Only goalies can use
their hands on the ball.
They have to stop the ball
any way they can.

Players can hit the ball with their heads. These are called headers.

Find Out More

BOOK
Hornby, Hugh. *Soccer*. New York: DK, 2010.

WEB SITE
Sports Illustrated Kids
www.sikids.com
This Web site has articles and videos about soccer.

Glossary

equipment (i-KWIP-muhnt) objects used to play a game

goalie (GOH-lee) the player who stays in the goal to stop the other team from scoring

popular (PAHP-yuh-lur) liked by many people

tournament (TUR-nuh-muhnt) a series of games in which a number of teams try to win the championship

Home and School Connection

Use this list of words from the book to help your child become a better reader. Word games and writing activities can help beginning readers reinforce literacy skills.

all	each	most	sport
almost	end	much	stop
are	every	names	teams
arms	field	need	tries
around	first	not	two
ball	four	other	use
big	goalies	pass	was
block	guards	people	with
can	hands	played	world
countries	may	shin	years

Index

About the Author

Joanne Mattern loves all sports. She loved playing soccer when she was in school. Joanne has written biographies of many athletes. She lives with her family in New York State.